PATRIOTIC SYMBOLS

The Lincoln Memorial

Nancy Harris

Heinemann Library
Chicago, Illinois

HEINEMANN-RAINTREE

TO ORDER:

☎ Phone Customer Service **888-454-2279**

🖥 Visit **www.heinemannraintree.com** to browse our catalog and order online.

Editorial: Rebecca Rissman
Design: Kimberly R. Miracle
Photo Research: Tracy Cummins and Tracey Engel
Production: Duncan Gilbert

Originated by Dot Gradations
Printed and bound in China by South China Printing Co. Ltd.
The paper used to print this book comes from sustainable resources.

ISBN-13: 978-1-4329-0966-6 (hc)
ISBN-10: 1-4329-0966-5 (hc)
ISBN-13: 978-1-4329-0973-4 (pb)
ISBN-10: 1-4329-0973-8 (pb)

12 11 10 09 08
10 9 8 7 6 5 4 3 2 1

Cataloging-in-Publication data avaiable at Library of Congress: loc.gov

Acknowledgments

The author and publisher are grateful to the following for permission to reproduce copyright material: ©Age Fotostock **p. 5** top left (Maurizio Borsari); ©Corbis **pp. 9, 20** (Bettmann); ©Getty Images **pp. 15, 17** (George Eastman House), **19** (Chris Pinchbeck); ©The Granger Collection, New York **p. 11**; ©Jupiter Images **p. 18** (Brand X Pictures); ©Library of Congress Prints and Photographs Division **pp. 10, 14**; ©Map Resources **p. 7**; ©North Wind Picture Archives **p. 12**; ©Shutterstock **pp. 4** (Stephen Finn), **5** top right (Arvind Balaraman), **5** bottom right (Raymond Kasprzak), **5** bottom left (ExaMedia Photography), **16** right (Cristina Ciochina), **16** left (Steve Broer); ©SuperStock **pp. 6, 23a** (Brand X), **8, 23b** (Timothy Hursley).

Cover image used with permission of ©Getty Images (Tim Brakefield). Back cover image used with permission of ©Shutterstock (Cristina Ciochina).

The publishers would like to thank Nancy Harris for her assistance in the preparation of this book.

Every effort has been made to contact copyright holders of any material reproduced in this book. Any omissions will be rectified in subsequent printings if notice is given to the publisher.

Disclaimer

All the Internet addresses (URLs) given in this book were valid at the time of going to press. However, due to the dynamic nature of the Internet, some addresses may have changed, or sites may have changed or ceased to exist since publication. While the author and publisher regret any inconvenience this may cause readers, no responsibility for any such changes can be accepted by either the author or the publisher.

Contents

What Is a Symbol?

The Lincoln Memorial is a symbol.
A symbol is a type of sign.

A symbol shows you something.

The Lincoln Memorial

The Lincoln Memorial is a special symbol.

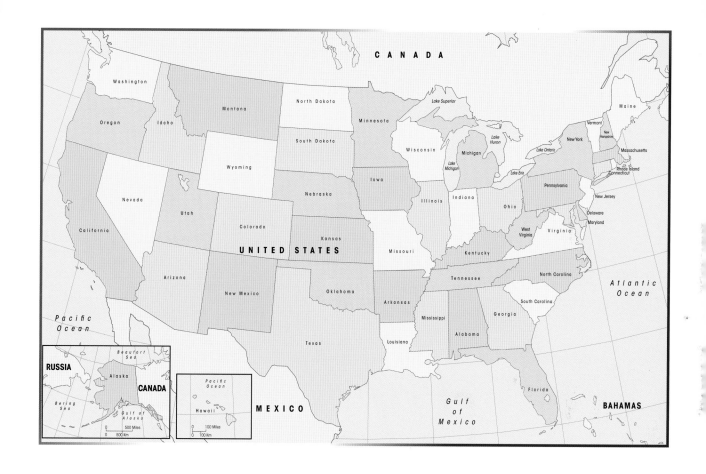

It is a symbol of the United States of America.
The United States of America is a country.

The Lincoln Memorial is a patriotic symbol.

It shows the beliefs of the country. It shows
how Lincoln is remembered as a great leader.

Abraham Lincoln

The Lincoln Memorial is a symbol of Abraham Lincoln. Lincoln was the 16th president.

There were slaves when Lincoln led the country. Slaves were not free to decide how they would live.

Lincoln wanted slaves to be free. The Lincoln Memorial is a symbol of how he helped free slaves.

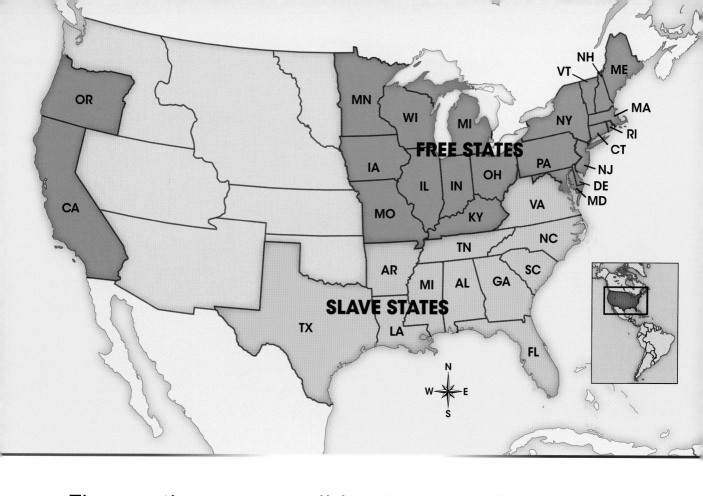

The southern states did not agree with Lincoln. The southern states did not want slaves to be free.

American Civil War

The northern states fought the southern states. The southern states did not want to be part of the country.

The Lincoln Memorial is a symbol of how Lincoln led the country. He led the states to come together.

The Memorial

The Lincoln Memorial looks like a temple. A statue of Abraham Lincoln is inside the memorial.

The memorial was built to honor Lincoln.
It is a symbol of how he supported freedom.

Columns

The Lincoln Memorial has 36 columns. There were 36 states when Lincoln led the country.

The columns are a symbol of the 36 states. They are a symbol of how Lincoln brought the states together.

What It Tells You

The Lincoln Memorial honors Abraham Lincoln for supporting freedom.

It reminds us of how he kept the country together.

Lincoln Memorial Facts

★ The Lincoln Memorial is in Washington, D.C.

★ The Lincoln Memorial was built between 1914 and 1922.

★ There were 48 states when the memorial was completed.

★ The names of the 48 states are on the outside of the memorial.

Glossary

memorial
something that reminds you of a person or event

patriotic
believing in your country

Index

Note to Parents and Teachers

The study of patriotic symbols introduces young readers to our country's government and history. Books in this series begin by defining a symbol before focusing on the history and significance of a specific patriotic symbol. Use the facts section on page 22 to introduce readers to these non-fiction features.

The text has been carefully chosen with the advice of a literacy expert to enable beginning readers success while reading independently or with moderate support. An expert in the field of early childhood social studies curriculum was consulted to provide interesting and appropriate content.

You can support children's nonfiction literacy skills by helping students use the table of contents, headings, picture glossary, and index.